FROGS

For James and the frog
in Rittenhouse Square—L.D.

For my nature-loving friend, Corey—J.M.

Cut-paper photography by Paul Dyer.

Special thanks to John Behler, Curator, Department of Herpetology, Wildlife Conservation Society, Bronx, NY.

ISBN 0-439-08645-0

Text copyright © 1998 by Laura Driscoll. Illustrations copyright © 1998 by Judith Moffatt.
All rights reserved.
Published by Scholastic Inc., 555 Broadway, New York, NY 10012,
by arrangement with Penguin Putnam Inc. SCHOLASTIC and associated logos are trademarks and/or registered trademarks of Scholastic Inc.

12 11 10 9 8 7 6 5 4 3 2 1   9/9 0 1 2 3 4/0

Printed in the U.S.A.   23

First Scholastic printing, April 1999

FROGS

By Laura Driscoll
Illustrated by Judith Moffatt

SCHOLASTIC INC.

New York Toronto London Auckland Sydney
Mexico City New Delhi Hong Kong

Ker-plunk!

Something splashes
into the pond.

A frog!
It has strong back legs.
It has webbed feet.
It swims fast.

Frogs feel at home
in the pond.
Why?
Because they begin life
in the water—
as tiny frog eggs.
In the spring,
a mother frog
lays lots of eggs.

The eggs hatch.

Frog babies swim out.

They look like fish.

They swim like fish.

They even breathe

underwater like fish.

But they are not fish.

They are tadpoles.

They will grow up to be frogs.

Soon the tadpoles change.
They get bigger.
They grow little back legs,
then front legs.

And little by little,
their tails shrink
and disappear!

Something also changes
inside them.
Now the baby frogs
can breathe out of the water,
like we do.

The frogs hop onto a log.

They are now land animals.

They still can swim.

But they are not
water animals anymore.

frog

Animals that change this way
are called <u>amphibians</u>.
(You say it like this:
am-FIH-bee-uns.)
Are frogs the only amphibians?

toad

No!

Toads are amphibians, too.

Toads usually have

bumpy skin and shorter legs

than frogs.

There are about 4,000
kinds of frogs.
They live all over the world.
Most frogs are
the size of your hand.

But the biggest frog
is called the Goliath frog,
like the giant.

This picture is about
the same size as the real frog.

21

Tree frogs are so tiny
they can stand
on your fingertip.
Can you guess
where tree frogs live?
In trees!
Their sticky toes
help them hold on tight!

Sometimes at night
you can hear tree frogs croak.
Lots of frogs croak.
They croak to find mates.

They also croak
to warn other frogs
of danger.
Many animals
like to eat frogs.

But these pretty frogs are safe.
Why doesn't the bird eat them?
Because they have poison
on their skin.

Snakes like to eat frogs.
But this Asian leaf frog is safe.
The snake cannot see it
in the pile of leaves.
The frog stays very still.
Soon the snake goes away.

The barking frog

fools its enemies another way.

It puffs itself up.

Now it looks too big to eat.

But most frogs in danger
do the same thing.
They hop away—fast!

Ker-plunk!